GW00702688

BREEDING
BRITISH BIRDS
IN AVIARIES AND CAGES

OTHER TITLES AVAILABLE
OR IN PRODUCTION

BREEDING
BRITISH BIRDS
IN AVIARIES AND CAGES

by
H. NORMAN

New Edition by
JAMES BLAKE

NIMROD PRESS LTD
15 The Maltings
Turk Street, Alton, Hampshire

This New and Enlarged Edition, 1988

ISBN 1-85259-137-4

Ptarmigan Printing

Publisher:
NIMROD PRESS LTD
15 The Maltings
Turk Street
Alton, Hampshire, GU34 1DL

INTRODUCTION

H. Norman was a leading expert on British Birds in aviculture and this small book was produced to cover the keeping and breeding of the most popular species. At the time of writing *The Protection of Birds Act* 1933 was in operation which made it illegal to keep birds in captivity unless close-ringed or bred in cage or aviary.

Since then the law has been strengthened the main statute being the *Wildlife and Countryside Act* 1981. Under that Act, British birds can only be acquired under licence and, if bred in captivity, there should be proof by means of a close ring (put on when the bird is very young) or by registration with an appropriate body such as the British Bird Council. In addition, any cages in which birds are kept should be sufficiently large enough to allow a bird to stretch its wings properly.

We all have a duty to keep birds in adequate housing and properly fed. As far as possible the food a bird eats naturally should be provided. However, as shown by the poultry industry, rabbit keeping and farm livestock, birds and animals can be kept in a very healthy state by providing the correct balance of protein, roughage, oils, calcium, and other essentials. The fact remains that these ·artificial foods are taken because the recipients have grown accustomed to them.

It is essential to recognize that British birds kept in aviaries fall into two categories:

1. **Seed Eaters** which belong mainly to the Finch family and eat various seeds.

2. **Softbills** consisting of Magpies, Jays, Jackdaws,

Thrushes, Blackbirds, Starlings, Larks, Pipits, Spotted Flycatchers, Hedge sparrows, Warblers, Nightingales and other similar species. These eat insects and various greenstuffs.

For success the food must be recognisable. If live insects are not available, the Softbills have to be given an acceptable alternative.

The law is constantly changing so the bird fancier should keep abreast of requirements by reading suitable journals such as *Cage and Aviary Birds* or *Feathered World*. This book indicates the present position, but if in doubt consult the experts.

A useful activity is membership of the local cage bird society, where members will be glad to give advice.

July, 1988

JAMES BLAKE

CONTENTS

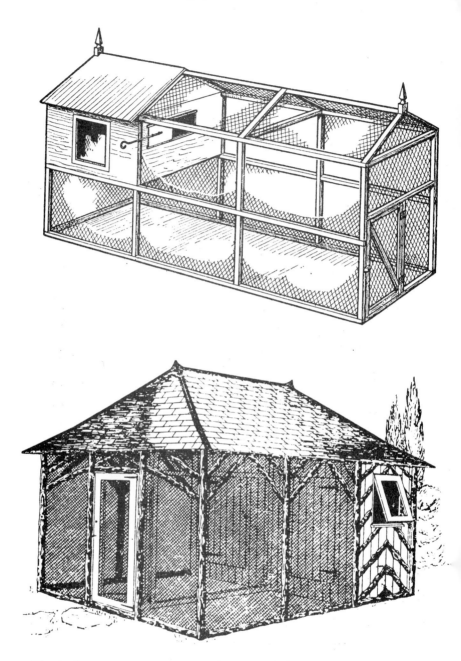

Typical Aviaries for British Birds — Minimum 6ft x 3ft x 6ft high, much larger for Softbills to breed.

BREEDING BRITISH BIRDS IN AVIARIES AND CAGES

CHAPTER I

HOUSING AND FOOD

Choosing the Accommodation : General Hints on Nesting and Feeding

EVER since the days of the ancient Egyptians wild birds have been caught and kept in cages and aviaries as pets for their song and beauty of plumage, and this pleasure-giving practice has continued, with variations as to keep and treatment, until the present time with very little restriction.

Now, however, if we desire these cheerful and happy songsters to enliven us and help to make us forget our everyday cares and troubles, we must build aviaries, or provide ourselves with special cages and offer the birds facilities to nest and rear young ones, thus keeping up the supply of songsters and exhibition specimens. Although the existing restrictions upon purchasing British birds tend to be irksome, the *Wildlife and Countryside Act,* 1981 (and amendments) will probably prove a blessing in the long run, and add additional pleasure and interest to the activities of British bird fanciers, who from now onwards will do more than just feed and attend to the everyday wants of their stock of native birds.

There will certainly be an added joy in watching the pairing, nesting and rearing of young, and after a time the fancier's spirit of emulation to breed and exhibit something better than his fellows—a specimen more choice in shape or colouring—is bound to show itself. In thus *breeding* winners there should be much more cause for pride than in the mere buying of the best that money can purchase.

I feel sure that in a few years we shall see a great improvement in the British birds section of our shows. The present-day varieties of Canaries are all descendants of the dowdy little green wild bird, and we have in Budgerigars a more recent example of what can be done by domestication and controlled breeding. Already aviary-bred Budgerigars are much larger and finer specimens than their wild Australian ancestors, to say nothing of the wonderful range of colours and regularity of markings evolved. All this has been accomplished in a few short years.

What has been done with Canaries and Budgerigars can be repeated with our lovely British birds. At first they may not nest so freely, but each season will be one step onward, and the further we get away from the wild-caught bird the easier the task will become, until eventually they will breed as freely as Canaries.

No New Idea

This breeding of our native species in aviaries and cages is no new idea. It has been carried on in a quiet manner for many years. I have myself at times had an odd pair or two of Finches nesting more or less successfully, and, of course, hybrid breeders have used Finch hens for the production of the beautiful crosses we see on the show bench. Thus there is no question about fanciers' ability to breed them, given suitable conditions.

The desire to reproduce their kind at certain seasons is present in all wild creatures, and our job is to give them suitable housing and to encourage and assist them to nest and rear young.

In order successfully to breed British birds there are three arrangements open to us in the way of accommodation. We can build outdoor or indoor aviaries, make large flights, or employ breeding cages. Aviaries, which may be of all sizes and shapes, can be placed in almost any situation, though naturally, with wild specimens, a certain amount of seclusion is an advantage.

A good many bird-keepers will, no doubt, favour a lean-to building because of its simplicity of design and erection. Most people have in their garden a boundary wall or fence and even if one cannot utilise this as it stands for one side or the back of the building, it offers something substantial to build against and thus means good, solid protection.

Now although an aviary can be of any size, it is desirable that it should not be less than eight or ten feet in length, since ample wing exercise is most essential. As a proof of how they enjoy this, fix up two perches, one at either end, as far apart as possible, and you will notice that all the birds use these perches in preference to others. This is especially true at certain times of the day, such as the late afternoon ; they will dart from one to the other as fast as they can fly.

Such exercise is good for them and keeps them strong and healthy, and therefore fit to perform the duties you require of them.

The height of the aviary in front should be five or six feet, with an extra foot at the back to allow a good fall of rain water from the roof. And in order that the interior shall not get wet there should be a good overlap of the roof beyond the walls of the building.

The Shelter

It is desirable that a certain portion of an aviary be boarded all round to serve as a shelter for the birds in bad weather, and as a hiding place when suddenly frightened. The inside of this shelter can be left open or boarded up about half way. Some are constructed with just a small opening between the shelter and the flight, in which case a window should be fixed to light up the interior, or the birds will not enter.

Boarding up about eighteen inches of the wired front and sides will prevent trouble from cats sitting on the ground close up against the wires, watching and alarming the birds. After a time the prowlers of the neighbourhood begin to realize that the aviary birds are not for them, and they pass along and take no further notice.

When fitting the perches in a span-roof aviary, the highest one, if fixed up near the extreme top of the roof, should be as long as possible. Birds roosting for the night all prefer the highest perch, and, consequently, if this is too short there will be a good deal of quarrelling. Bickering, once started, is apt to continue, and as it is peace that one wants in a breeding aviary one should be careful not to do anything that is likely to cause trouble.

Some may prefer an aviary with a large open flight, and there is, of course, no real objection to this. It should be boarded round the bottom, and wire netting of not less than half-inch mesh used to cover it. All seed hoppers and feeding vessels should be placed under cover.

In my opinion an aviary should not be of open wire all round. I have never yet seen one so built that was a complete success, the owner having (generally at some trying period) to cover up part of it with sacking or tarpaulin material, which is seldom a success and certainly not particularly sightly. Although one might argue that birds at liberty are exposed to all the winds that blow, they are able to move about and gain shelter from shrubs and trees, a thing they are quite unable to do when confined.

In newly-erected aviaries all woodwork should be treated before it is covered with wire. Some may like to use paint of a particular shade, but a preservative such as Solignum is much better, and can be obtained in many colours. If a plain dark brown is not objected to, creosote looks well and preserves the wood, and, if put on hot, penetrates and dries quickly. A little Stockholm tar can be added to creosote with advantage; it gives more " body " and improves the preserving qualities.

The Aviary Floor

The floor of an aviary is a matter that needs a good deal of consideration. If the whole structure is to be raised off the ground, a few joists across, and floor boards nailed to them, make an excellent clean base that can be covered with sand or sawdust. The whole structure can then be raised a foot or so from the ground and supported by bricks at each corner. If the aviary is a fixture, concrete makes the soundest and cleanest floor, and one that can be scraped, brushed, or be given a periodical scrub.

The concrete need not be of a great thickness ; if the earth is well rammed down, an inch of cement put on smoothly will be quite sufficient. Broken glass mixed with the earth prevents vermin burrowing underneath, while if ordinary earth mixed with glass is used for the floor it should be well rammed down until quite smooth, and then covered with a good thick layer of sand and sawdust, or a mixture of sand and coconut fibre. Wherever possible, however, I urge a concrete floor. It is sanitary, and the aviary may stand in the same position for years. With an earth floor, the soil must occasionally be renewed or the aviary moved to a fresh site when the floor becomes foul.

Flights and Miniature Aviaries

" Flights " or " flight cages " are actually small aviaries, or very large cages. These, like an aviary, can be of any size, but the usual dimensions are about four to six feet long and two feet from back to front. They can be placed outdoors in sheltered situations, raised a couple of feet or more from the ground ; or they may be fixed up in a spare room in the house, or out in the garden in an open shed. An ingenious development of this scheme is the " miniature aviary " invented and popularised by Mr. Percy Glover. Invaluable where space is limited, this arrangement gives the birds almost every advantage of the normal aviary. Ordinary flight cages, exposed to the weather, would quickly become ruined, but the little aviaries in question will withstand all conditions. Each section is intended for a pair of birds.

A large open shed outdoors, with a wire front to it is probably the best and most successful method of housing prospective breeding Finches. They get plenty of light and air, and when accommodated in pairs are easily managed. Although two pairs might be allowed in a large flight, a single pair will do better. The food supply for one species is not always the best for another, and obviously one should try to adopt the method that offers the greater chance of success.

Nearly all of our British cage birds have at various times been bred in ordinary breeding cages. These should not be less than about 36 inches in length with a sliding partition, either in the centre, or, better still, making two compartments of unequal size. There are times when it may be advisable to part the pair for a short period.

In both flights and cages, the seed, food and water vessels should be so placed that they do not become fouled, and can be easily refilled without undue disturbance to the birds.

The manner of furnishing the aviary and flights for British bird breeding is a matter that requires a little careful attention. If we can make our aviary resemble as far as possible the wild birds' natural surroundings we shall encourage and please them, and advance one step nearer our goal.

This can be done by buying some tile battens from the wood yard (this timber is quite cheap) and nailing lengths against the walls, about a foot apart, from top to bottom. Then fasten to this some ordinary chicken-run wire netting. Clumps of heather, furze and box trees can now be twisted into the wire in the corners and suitable places.

Fix them in bunches, to make miniature trees or bushes, in which the birds will probably build. If the aviary is of fair size quite big bunches or faggots can be fastened and made secure with string or wire. This can be done both in the open flight and in the covered portion. Should a pair select a bush in the open for nesting it is a simple matter to give them a little protection by quietly laying a board on the wire immediately above the nest, putting a large stone or weight on it so that it cannot be moved by the wind.

Encouragement to Breed

Although spring is the normal nesting-time for all birds, in confinement they may need a little encouragement. Some will start building right away in a bush, or bunch of branches, as they would in the open, but the majority need something to begin with. We can hang ordinary Canary nest pans in odd places, and we can do the same with nest boxes.

A Small Flight

Soaking Seeds

These latter one can make of various sizes, four, five and even six inches in width and breadth ; a handful of moss or short hay can be put into them and worked round in the shape of a nest. The birds will pull some of this out and scatter it about, but that does not matter since it shows that they are interested and later will start collecting material with a definite object.

Another nesting receptacle is the common German Canary travelling cage with a few of the bars cut out, so that the bird can easily enter. Some twigs of heather should be twisted among the bars to give seclusion and a semblance of wild surroundings. In the past one could purchase wicker-work nests, but I have not seen any lately. If these are still procurable they will be admirable for the purpose.

Old wild birds' nests of any species are valuable ; they are taken to readily. If they are Thrushes' or Blackbirds' nests and you need them for Finches, put a handful of moss or hay in the bottom to give them a start. Old Finch nests, however much they are broken, can be used, and one can work a little material in something of the outward shape of a nest with some rough material and fix it in one of the bushes.

Nest Boxes

Birds such as Starlings should have a nest box with an entrance at the side ; in fact in a large aviary one or two of these could be fixed up irrespective of the species of bird kept. I once had a hen Bullfinch that built in one and a Greenfinch that built in a flower-pot. One never knows just what our native birds will do when confined and domesticated ; part of their wild nature has gone, and with it some of their natural, wild ways.

When using cages for breeding a short length of wood should be fixed across one corner and a bunch of heather or shrub be pushed into the angle. A nest pan thrust amongst these twigs will give the hen a start.

There are other gadgets that will suggest themselves to keen bird breeders, and I do not know of anything more intcresting and pleasurable than to see a hen Bullie taking to something that we have arranged specially for her. To watch her building the nest is particularly interesting, for her actions are quite different from those of a Canary.

Although I propose to deal with the feeding of each species separately, a few general notes on the subject will not be out of place. We have a most valuable collection of seeds for our birds as supplied in a clean, dry state by the seed merchants. What with Canary, Hemp, Rape, Teazle, Niger and Linseed, one would think nothing else was needed, but of these valuable seeds there are only Rape, Linseed and Teazle that the birds would be able to obtain in the fields, and actually Rape and its near relatives Charlock and Wild Mustard are the only kinds at all plentiful.

In their natural state British Finches live on seeds from wild plants that we call weeds, growing in the fields and waste land, the berries of the hedgerows, and insect life generally. Although the seeds we purchase will keep Finches in good condition and song, we need them to be in high fettle for breeding purposes, and few realize the difference between birds that are healthy and in song and those in really high breeding condition.

I have many times seen a cock Linnet sitting comfortably on a swaying branch and singing his delightful song without any signs of emotion. Another, not far away, may be in genuinely high fettle, fairly dancing on his perch, his wings flapping, his throat swelling and his song pouring out for all he is worth.

"High Condition"

There is the difference. The second bird is in high breeding condition, the condition in which we want our birds to be when they go to nest. To get them like this we must follow nature as closely as we are able. Those bird keepers who live in the country can collect bunches of useful stuff without much trouble, and suburban dwellers will find many plants growing on allotments and bare patches, and possibly a limited number in their own garden.

The real town man is somewhat handicapped, but he can get from the seedsman several valuable seeds, such as Sesame, Gold of Pleasure, Dandelion, Thistle, Cornflower, Lettuce, and one or two others, and with these he can make a valuable mixture.

In addition to these, some firms put up an excellent wild seed mixture which they have obtained from farmers' threshings, and, after screening and re-screening to eliminate all the dirt and dust, are able to offer it to bird keepers as an additional food for their pets. Some of these mixtures are splendid for the Finches, containing as they do many choice seeds that could be obtained in no other way. They can be purchased in packets and in 7 lb. and 14 lb. bags, and although not cheap the seed is well worth the price usually asked for it.

Soaked Seed

Another food that can be given with advantage is soaked seed. This can be used by everybody, but is particularly valuable to those bird keepers who are unable to obtain half-ripe seeding wild food.

Dry seeds should be soaked for 36 hours in cold water, the water being frequently changed. It should then be strained off as dry as possible, and, if this is done overnight, and the strainer stood on one side just tilted a little, the seed will be in a good condition to be used in the morning. To keep up a constant supply two or three basins should be kept going.

If the seed is required in a hurry and there is not time to drain it thoroughly, a spoonful of dry biscuit meal or prepared food can be mixed with it to dry up the superfluous moisture. Sprouted seeds also provide valuable food.

Although it is possible to rear birds on seeds and bunches of seeding wild food gathered in the open, it is necessary to supply the parent birds with some kind of soft food, because our wild plants may fail us at a critical time, and there are some who cannot get them. If the Finches can be induced to take soft food it simplifies matters considerably.

Whatever soft food we decide to use, the birds should be got accustomed to it some time before they start nesting ; it is folly to wait until the young have arrived before supplying it.

If the birds do not take to the food, a little should be mixed in a small supply of seed fresh daily, but after a time it can be given separately.

The question arises as to what soft food should be given to assist the birds in the rearing of the young. Naturally the first we consider is hard-boiled chickens' eggs, as being the nearest meaty food to insect life. All the yolk can be used with about one-third of the white, which should be mixed with powdered Osborne biscuits or brown breadcrumbs.

The latter is to be preferred to white bread, and the birds seem to like it better. As a proof of this, if you place a small heap of each of them out in the open you will notice that the Chaffinches, Hedge Sparrows, Thrushes and Blackbirds prefer the brown, and even those greedy birds the House Sparrows will eat the brown first.

For those bird breeders who do not care to use hard-boiled egg, there are some good, ready-made foods upon the market. These are excellent and most useful if the birds are trained to eat them. But the food I like best, one that has been used successfully for the rearing of British birds, mules and hybrids, is a superior brand of insectile food as used for the feeding of British and Foreign Warblers.

The best of these foods will rear the most delicate youngsters. Fresh egg food is, no doubt, of great value, and even when using insectile mixture as a stock food, a little can be given occasionally as a change. But one should be very careful with it, because when given in any quantity regularly it does not seem quite to suit British hardbills.

When Finches are once on soft food it is not difficult to get them to take a small portion of bread dipped in milk, and this, besides acting as a splendid corrective, affords splendid nourishment for the young.

Colour Feeding Seedeaters

Colour feeding is practised by some exhibitors, but care is necessary in selecting which species to treat. There are differences of opinion, but generally the Green or Yellow colours are excluded. On the other hand many birds with red colouring may be improved; these include Redbills, Bullfinches, Buntings, Bramblings and Chaffinches.

The method usually employed is to add to the water or food when the birds are moulting. The Carophyll Red is mixed with boiling water (sufficient to cover 1-penny piece to two pints of water) and then used as drinking water for a number of days each week. Some fanciers advise against too strong a mixture or too frequent use — two or three days a week is usually sufficient.

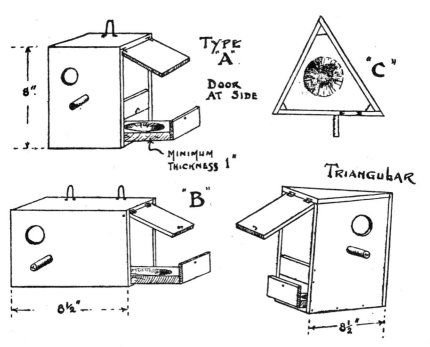

Typical Nest-boxes which may be used for British Birds

CHAPTER II

THE GOLDFINCH *

Hybrids : The Nest : Sex Distinctions : Food

OF all our natural cage birds, the Goldfinch is undoubtedly the most popular. He is bright and
cheerful, has an attractive song, and is gay in plumage,
with some very effective splashes of bright colour about him.

His red face is quite distinct from any of the other
Finches, and although some of them can boast an edging
of pure yellow in the wings, none of them are quite so
brilliant and plentiful. He is well named " Goldiewing "
and " Goldspark " by country people.

We not only value the Goldfinch for his own sake as a
songster and exhibition bird, but he has proved his useful-
ness as a producer of beautiful mules both dark and light
in plumage, and of wonderful hybrids when crossed with
other Finches. He is so valuable as a fancier's bird that
we cannot do without him, and now to retain him we
must definitely breed our own specimens, for the British
Goldfinch is protected all the year round in all counties.

Fortunately, he is a bird that takes well to domesticated
life ; he is quite at home in aviary, flight, or cage, and
has bred frequently in all such quarters—not only with
his own species, but when crossed with Canaries and other
British Finches for the production of hybrids.

The hens, if in good condition, will nest readily in nest
boxes, pans, or wicker cages, and will build a beautiful
nest, sometimes taking an old wild bird's home as a
foundation. The nest is a compact, closely built structure,
with a good strong felted rim, and to encourage her to
make this we must supply her with the most suitable
material, letting her take her choice and go about the

*See *Cage Bird Hybrids*, Charles Houlton for details of hybrid breeding

building in her own way without any interference from her owner.

I have a nest in front of me composed of moss, fine roots, and dry grass stems, the outer structure being joined together with bits of lichen and spiders' webs. It is neatly lined inside with feathers, vegetable down and hair.

Nearly all these materials we can supply without much difficulty. The fine roots we can find on the edge of a field or allotment, or we can pull up by the roots some coarse grass or herbage and lay it on the roof of the aviary to dry before putting it inside.

Moss we can gather or purchase in bunches at the nearest nurseryman's; dry grass stems should be broken into odd lengths; vegetable down we must hunt for, and we shall find it in waste places on old Thistle stems, Ragwort and Goat's-Beard, also in neglected gardens on old plants that have not been cut down.

Cow-hair will not give us any trouble. We can easily get that either from the bird shops or in quantity from dealers who advertise aviary requisites. The nest pans, boxes and so on should be fixed in position some time before they are required, to give the birds the opportunity to examine them and to make their selection.

Giving the Nest Material

The building materials can wait until there are some signs of nesting by the birds, that is to say, when the cock or hen is observed playing with a bit of dry material. As soon as this is noticed a supply of the coarser kinds can be given, followed by others as the building progresses.

When the hen has laid and begun to sit, she should not be interfered with; many a clutch of eggs has been spoilt by the bird's owner taking too great an interest in her doings.

She will incubate about 13 days, and the behaviour of the pair will soon give one some clue as to what has happened. Supply soft food, a little soaked Teazle and wild food and leave them as much as possible to themselves to get on with the job. As the young ones grow, increase the supply of the food of which the parents make most use.

Goldfinches are rather late in going to nest, and the very late ones frequently have only one nest ; but with a good supply of proper food a second nest can be expected.

Some bird keepers experience difficulty in distinguishing the sexes of Goldfinches. Generally speaking they are very much alike, and there is not the distinction in colour that exists in some species. Cock birds have rather longer heads and are somewhat flat on the crown, with stoutish beaks. If the bird is caught and the wing is opened the butt is jet black with a greenish flush when caught by the light. Turn him over on his back and one can see a decided yellow tinge on the breast. The red blaze of the face runs well back past the eye.

TYPICAL GOLDFINCHES

The longer and " flatter " head of the cock (lower) is clearly shown here

The head of the hen is somewhat rounder with a rather less stout beak, and the butts of the wings have a brownish tinge to them.

The feeding of Goldfinches is a matter that requires careful attention as so much depends upon the condition of the birds to secure success. Most fanciers have their own special seed mixtures, and although these vary in the proportions of the ingredients, the same seeds are nearly always included.

The following is a mixture that will keep most Finches in good condition :—Teazle seed 4 parts, Canary 3 parts, Hemp 2 parts, and Linseed 1 part. Then to provide variety and assist condition one can give a little Thistle, Dandelion, Maw, Cornflower, and chopped walnuts, and a few Sunflower seeds.

Our greatest aids to condition, and in keeping the birds in health during the nesting and rearing of the young, are the wild food and seeding plants we can collect in the open. One of the first is Dandelion, of which we can use both the leaves and ripening seed pods, and before this is finished we have Sow-Thistle, another plant that can be used in both ways. Then follow in quick succession Chickweed, Shepherd's-Purse, seeding grasses and a host of others.

A supply of these should be collected two or three times a week and given to the birds until the young arrive, and they should then be offered daily. It is by variety in food, and attention to their wants without fussing, that success is ensured.

When the young can feed themselves, soft food, soaked seeds and sprouted seeds should be supplied until they are well on to the usual seed mixture.

Judging the Goldfinch

The Goldfinch should be judged on the basis of its cardinal features:

1. Size — the larger bird is to be preferred. The standard size

is around 4½ ins.

2. Type — a bold, jaunty bird full of vigour and with a nice shape is essential. Head broad with strong bill.

3. Colour — deep and rich colours are necessary:

(a) Head — red should be deep and brilliant and white band should be as clear as possible,

(b) Body — rich brown on shoulders and breast; white on lower part of breast.

(c) Wings and Tail — black with yellow bars, deep and rich in colour.

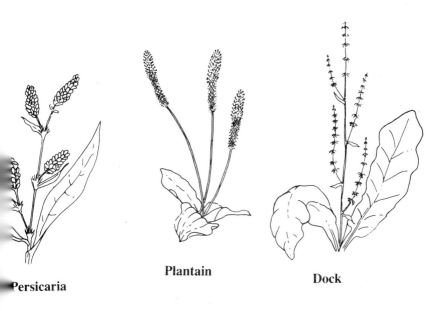

Persicaria

Plantain

Dock

Green Food

Bullfinch
Keep only one pair in the aviary — they are very pugnacious

CHAPTER III

THE BULLFINCH

"Improving the Breed" : Foster Parents
Seclusion : Conditioning

HERE we have another prime favourite cage bird, a bold, handsome, showy specimen very typical of his name. Although not much of a songster, his shape and beautiful colouring and his contented disposition, whether in cage or aviary, have always made him very much sought after as a drawing-room pet, aviary inmate, and exhibition bird.

Now that we are going to breed Bullfinches in quantity, in aviaries and cages, we shall, no doubt, in a few seasons note a great improvement in size, shape and colour, and as they will probably be free breeders when paired together (instead of to another species, which has hitherto been the usual lot of the hen) we shall soon possess substantial aviary-bred stocks.

Young hens are to be preferred as they are almost certain nesters, and take to the ordinary nest pan or box without much trouble. Occasionally we may have one that does not, and then it becomes necessary to use any device that will encourage her. I feel sure that, when the birds drop their eggs on the floor of the flight or cages, it is because they are not quite satisfied with their nesting arrangements.

The Bullfinch hen is a very prolific layer of eggs, and sometimes clutches follow too quickly. Where this is the case some of them can be transferred to Canaries or other foster parents. Although the hen has a rather bad reputation for sitting and rearing, we must not forget that her partner has usually been a cock of another species, and it is just possible that they will act better when paired up in a natural manner. I have known several pairs that have done well.

Bullfinches in a wild state pair for life and are very devoted and constant to each other. This being the case it is as well to start with young birds, and while healthy keep the same pair together. Although the hen in captivity will build with almost anything reasonably suitable that comes to hand, it is as well to supply her with the correct materials such as fine twigs, roots and hair, to which can be added a scrap of wool and a few feathers.

When nesting, the hen is shy and retiring, and whatever nest we use (either pan or box) it should be somewhat secluded. This can be managed by the arrangement of a few twigs of heather or shrub. Possibly a sheet of brown paper or cardboard can be tacked in the right position to give added privacy.

In a wild state the food of the Bullfinch consists of the buds of fruit and other trees, wild seeds, and berries. A good seed mixture can be made up from two parts of Canary and Teazle, with a half part each of Linseed, Rape, and Charlock. A few Sunflower seeds may be supplied daily. Hemp seed is not good for them and if used it should be given only very sparingly.

A spoonful of wild seed mixture will help to get them into condition, and then in the early spring we can offer budding twigs of fruit and hawthorn, Dandelion, Shepherd's-Purse, Sow-Thistle, Chickweed, and many others as they come into season. The fruit and berries of the garden can be offered during the summer months.

These items must be freely supplied when the young are about, not forgetting the various seeding grasses which are so valuable when old birds are rearing, and which will often induce them to feed when they are slacking off.

The novice should have no difficulty whatever in sexing these birds, as only the cock has the red breast. The sex of young Bullfinches in their nest feathers can easily be ascertained by the removal of two or three breast feathers, as the new ones will show the red of the cock if they are of that sex. When breeding, an enclosure should not contain more than one pair of Bullfinches, as the hens are very quarrelsome.

Judging Bullfinches

The remarks on Goldfinches are also applicable here. Features to watch are:

1. Size — around 6 ins. in size with a quite rounded body and broad head and neck.

2. Colours — brilliant colours with a black head, salmon/crimson breast, with grey shoulders and white around the vent and on wing band.

Chickweed — a great favourite

Linnets

CHAPTER IV

THE LINNET

A Songster : Breeding Sites : Trusting the Cock Wild Seed

IT is doubtful if any other of our native birds has achieved a popularity equal to that of the Linnet as a singing pet. He is not a particularly attractive bird as far as appearance goes, but as a songster he is the sweetest of them all, and when in condition he will sing the whole of the long summer's day.

So popular is he too for singing contests and exhibitions that we cannot afford to lose him as a cage and aviary bird. Although of a rather nervous disposition he takes kindly to domestication and quickly settles down to enjoy his life with the good things around him.

Linnets are free breeders and will produce two or three nests during the season. A pair properly mated become devoted to each other and should not be parted while they remain in health.

In an aviary or large flight open to the air, the hen will take to a nest box, or rough foundation for a nest placed in a clump of gorse and heather, and will build a most charming nest equal to that of any Finch for beauty of construction. When filled with the clutch of reddish spotted eggs it makes a delightful picture.

The cock can be safely trusted with the eggs and is attentive to the sitting hen. Although she is a close sitter and not easily disturbed, it is as well to pretend not to see her when attending to the daily wants, for however tame she is one cannot treat a wild-bred Finch quite as we do the domesticated Canary.

For building the nest, we must supply a few very fine birch twigs, grass stalks, moss, a few small feathers, hair, vegetable down, and a little wool.

I have seen the cock assisting the hen in the construction of the nest and between them they make a cosy home.

I do not think there are any of our Finches that feed so generally upon seeds as does the Linnet and, when at liberty, Rape, Charlock and Wild Mustard form the principal food, although many others are included as they come into season and ripen.

When caged we must not overdo the Rape and Charlock, as these seeds if given alone cause the birds to be rather loose in the bowels. A mixture should be made up as follows :—3 parts of Canary, 2 parts of Teazle, and 1 part of each of Rape, Charlock and Linseed.

This makes a splendid staple mixture, and we can give them variety by offering a little genuine wild seed mixture, and occasionally a little Gold of Pleasure, Niger, Plantain, Sesame and Thistle and a few grains of sound Hemp.

Soaked Seeds

Linnets are rather difficult birds to get on to soft food ; some, indeed, will not look at it, so that feeding them when they have young ones is not an easy matter. To get over this difficulty we must rely mostly upon soaked seeds, some of them just soaked and strained off, others allowed to sprout.

If possible bunches of wild food should be gathered. The favourites are Chickweed and Shepherd's-Purse, the latter collected very carefully so as not to scatter the ripe seeds near the root of the plant. Groundsel, seeding grass, Wild Mustard and many others can be included.

To most people the sexes in Linnets are alike in general appearance, but to the eye of a fancier there is a fairly pronounced difference. Cocks are generally bolder and fuller about the head, richer in colour, especially upon the back ; the breast and body markings are rather different ; and if the bird is caught, laid on its back, and the breast feathers turned up with a pencil, the cocks will show a reddish moon near the edge of each feather.

The hen does not have this dark mooning but each feather shows a distinct stripe down the centre. Some fanciers will tell you that the cocks have whiter primary feathers in the wings, but I do not think this is reliable. I have seen some hens with a greater display of white than many cocks.

Judging Linnets

The Linnet is not such a heavyweight and, therefore, must be judged as being a more peaceful bird than the heavier finches.

In size the Linnet is around 5½ inches long (male bird).

Points to watch are:

1. Size — a nicely proportioned bird with no exaggerated features.

2. Colour — basically a deep brown bird with head a slate-grey/ brown. The head and breast may have red markings — these vary according to the environment and age of the bird.

3. Feathering — should be close and fine.

B

Greenfinch

CHAPTER V

THE GREENFINCH

Early and Late Breeders : A Nest Box is Better : Sexing—A Point to Note

I FIRMLY believe that the bold Greenfinch is the commonest bird we have in the open fields and hedgerows. A proof of this lies in a day's birds'-nesting in open country where there are hedges and small plantations, for although one may find nests of many species, perhaps a colony of Linnets or several Chaffinches, none of them will compare with the number of Greenfinches that can be located.

These birds nest early and late. We can find them in the spring when there is scarcely sufficient foliage to hide the nest, and we can see them in late autumn, even after the harvest has been gathered and the fields are bare ; and each brood of four or five youngsters is generally safely reared.

Although the Greenfinch is not notable for his song, he has been a popular cage bird for many generations. It has usually been a brood of " Green Linnets " with which the country schoolboy has made his first attempts at hand rearing, and no lustier or stronger birds could be selected for the purpose.

It will be no hardship for the fancier and bird lover to breed Greenfinches, as these birds nest easily in aviaries, flights and cages. After a few years' breeding one can

*Obviously no longer permitted

imagine the great improvement brought about by breeders—improvement in size, colour, and shape. Besides, there is always the possibility of a break in the plumage under domestication, that would soon give us variegated, marked, and clear specimens.

No wild bird to my knowledge will breed quite so freely in an aviary or flight as a pair of tame Greenfinches. If well fed and looked after they will be the first to nest in the spring, and continue to do so right through the summer until the autumn moult.

One pair that I kept did so well that I had as many Greenies as I could manage, so I turned them out in the late summer months. I thought they had finished, but they built one more nest in the branches of a climbing plant almost touching the roof of the building, and still looked for their share of the soft food when the others were being fed.

Old wicker cages, or an old wild bird's nest, tucked away in a bush, will be preferred by the hens as nesting sites, although they will build in anything. Alternatively the " foundation " can be fixed up in a bundle of furze or broom.

Preference for a Nest Box

When breeding with Greenfinches in a cage, give them a nest box in preference to a pan and let it be of good size, say about six inches square, so that there is room in it for a good wad of rough nesting material.

Hang the box fairly high up, quite half-way, and put it at the most secluded end of the cage, if necessary masking the top part of the cage front with paper or cardboard. These precautions are not absolutely necessary in all cases, but they help towards success and anyway are not much trouble.

When building their nests in the open, Greenfinches are not so particular about the material they use as are some hardbills. It is not often that we can find two nests quite alike, and if we do it is because some particular substance is very common in the district. As an instance, I found two nests not far from each other, both of which were composed almost entirely of hay—quite an unusual occurrence, as hay is mostly used with other material.

In most cases Greenfinches will build a rather large nest for their size, composed of twigs, coarse roots, dry grass, and a little moss. The interior is of good shape and finished off quite neatly (for such a clumsy bird) with finer roots, a little wool, hair and feathers.

If our aviary specimens are supplied with moss, short lengths of grass with the roots attached, hair, cotton wool and a few feathers, they will put together quite a good nest.

The Greenfinch is a rather gross feeder and probably one of the easiest birds to cater for, but like all others he responds to good treatment. In a wild state he is mostly a seed eater with a taste for newly-sown wheat and oats, and liking a good share of the harvest in the autumn ; but at other times he clears the land of Charlock, Dock, Wild Mustard, grass seed and many others. As a staple food we can offer him Canary, Rape and Teazle ; the best mixture is as much Canary as the other two put together.

Occasional Seeds

Occasionally he can have a little Linseed and Hemp, and Sunflower seed almost daily, especially if he should be located in an aviary when the extra exercise will counteract the fattening properties of this seed.

A pinch of good wild seed mixture makes a change. Then there are the berries of the hedgerow, seeding wild food, and plants, all of which will be picked over and help to keep him healthy and fit.

When nesting all these varieties can be given, as well as some kind of soft food. As regards this he will not give us much trouble, taking almost anything offered to him, but such food should be of fairly good quality and not just rough chicken meal.

I know some pairs have reared young on the latter, and although they were lusty youngsters they would probably have been better had they been brought up on more digestible food.

Soaked and sprouting Hemp and Sunflower seeds are good and half-ripe ears of corn will be eagerly taken. A fancier could grow some of this in the corner of his own garden if Sparrows and other wild birds were not too plentiful.

Young Greenies are lusty feeders and the parents should be well supplied with food, particularly in the early morning and about four o'clock in the afternoon, when they start feeding in earnest after a midday slackening off.

The bird keeper should have no trouble in distinguishing the sexes of Greenfinches, since as a rule the hen is not so large and is much duller in plumage. The yellow in the wing of the cock is more pronounced than in the hen, her outer primary feathers being only edged with yellow.

There is more yellowish coloration in the plumage of the cock, the hen's feathering being mostly a dull, greenish brown. Young Greenfinches resemble their mother in general plumage, but the cocks are usually the larger, with a bolder look especially about the head and beak, and brighter colour in the wing bars.

After the moult, of course, they have their adult plumage, which simplifies the matter of sexing them because we have others from the same brood, and, comparing one with the other, we can decide which are the cocks.

This is a matter of some importance because we may get young cocks in one brood very little brighter in colour than some of the hens in another ; but in the same brood the distinction is usually more apparent.

Judging Greenfinches

The question of size is important and so is the colour, thus.

1. Size — 6ins long with a strong thick-set body with a thick powerful bill.
2. Colour — the general colour is olive-yellow shading to lighter colours. An older bird will show more colour and is to be preferred.
3. Condition — this is vital and should be reflected in a fit bird with wings carried tight to the body.

As with other species, clean well groomed birds are essential.

CHAPTER VI

THE CHAFFINCH

Interesting Crosses : Friendliness : Sprouting Seed and Insectile Mixtures

ALTHOUGH the Chaffinch has not been of much use to breeders for the production of mules and hybrids—only about three genuine hybrids having been recorded—these rarities have, as may be imagined, proved particularly interesting.

The crosses evolved have been Chaffinch-Bramblefinch, Chaffinch-Greenfinch and Chaffinch-Siskin, though in my life experience of cage bird shows I have only seen a single specimen of the last-named cross, though others may, possibly, have been produced. Anyway we hope to see more, and to get them we must do our best to retain the Chaffinch parent.

As a cage bird and songster he is one of the gayest. His plumage is conspicuously bright, and when in breeding condition with his blue cap and ruddy breast he is particularly attractive and intelligent, has a lively manner and usually greets his attendant with a cheerful note.

One cannot consider the Chaffinch to be a high-class songster, and yet, years ago, they used to figure at singing contests. Now they are out of favour, the great increase in the Roller Canary singing contests having probably turned their sport-loving owners' attention in another direction.

Still, Master Chaffie is very popular as an exhibition bird and a few of them are nearly always to be seen at the smallest shows.

It is not only the cock that is prized as a show bird, the hen of recent years having come very much into favour. She makes quite a successful exhibit in a mixed class for hens, with her sleek plumage and bright manner, without being quite so fidgety as the cock.

That being so, we have a double purpose in view when breeding this species, for we may turn out winners of both sexes, and, of course, all are useful for breeding purposes the following year.

Chaffinches have been reared both in aviaries and cages. The cock is an ardent and attentive partner, while the hen is most adaptable, and if well treated gets quite " chummy " with her owner, and is always on the look out for a special tit-bit, mealworm or spider, which she accepts with a delighted " pink, pink ".

THE CHAFFINCH

The breeder who will take pains to get his hens, of whatever species, on friendly terms with him, stands a much greater chance of success than one who does not take this trouble. Most hens, undoubtedly, respond to good treatment and it is an added pleasure to see how trustful they become.

When at liberty the Chaffinch builds the most compact and charming nest of all the Finches ; it is of the felted type, strong and well put together.

I have located scores of nests of this variety in my time, and been struck by the diversity of the materials used in building them. Whatever they are made of they are always skilfully finished.

A Breeding Hint

If one has a choice I would advise that a pair of these birds be provided with a large flight cage to themselves in an outside building as the cock is inclined to be pugnacious in the breeding season.

In a big aviary where the pairs have lived amicably together during the winter they should do well ; but it is when birds in high condition are thrown suddenly together that trouble usually occurs.

An old wicker cage or nest box fixed up and partly hidden with foliage would be most likely to start them building. The materials for the purpose should be moss of various kinds in plenty, dry grass, fine roots, a little wool, a scrap or two of paper, feathers, hair and vegetable down.

The hen is the builder while the cock fusses round. They take several days to complete the nest, adding a bit now and again, until one wonders if they mean business or not. As a new nest is made for each brood it is as well to fix up more than one cage or nest box before the season actually starts. The hen is a close sitter and not easily disturbed.

The food of the Chaffinch is mostly seeds and small insects. He is rather a dainty feeder and appears to prefer the seeds softened and sprouted. In the spring he makes himself rather a nuisance to the gardener when his seeds have just begun to swell. This fondness of his for sprouting seeds we must not forget, and by keeping Rape, Turnip and Radish seeds moist and warm for a few days we have an ideal food for this species and one that is particularly useful when they are feeding young.

If sown thickly and allowed to get well started it can be cut out in squares and both the roots and growth given to the birds. As a stock food I like the following mixture : Canary and Teazle 4 parts of each ; Rape, Charlock and Linseed 1 part of each. A few Sunflower seeds can be given daily and a small feed of Hemp provided once a week.

A mealworm or two and other live food must be provided, especially in the spring and summer months. They will eat live ants' eggs, smooth caterpillars, grubs, earwigs, spiders, green fly, gentles, wasp grubs, etc.

During the winter the old birds can have an occasional feed of mashed walnuts, which take the place of the beech nuts they would get if at liberty.

Chaffinches are not particularly keen on green food, but all the well-known plants should be offered, such as Chickweed, Shepherd's-Purse, Groundsel, Dandelion and so on. These should be gathered very carefully and given in bunches ; the birds will look them over keenly and find many tiny insects among them.

The best soft food is a good brand of insectile mixture made moist, although I have had them eat it dry. A small portion of finely-chopped suet can sometimes be added to it when insects are scarce—Atora Shredded Suet is ideal for this purpose.

The soft food should be offered to them some time before they go to nest, so that they will take it freely when needed.

Even a beginner should have no trouble in distinguishing the sexes, the cock alone having the ruddy coloured breast and the bluish cap. The hen is quite soberly clad but shows the Chaffinch wing with the white shoulder patch. She is shy and retiring in her manner compared with the cock.

Judging the Chaffinch

The chaffinch is a bright perky bird and this fact should be reflected in his or her attitude in the show pen. In size it is around 5¾ ins in length.

Show points are:

1. Size — a bold, sizeable bird.

2. Age — at least one year old to get the bright colour.

3. Feathering — tight and smooth and without any imperfections.

The male chaffinch is a very attractive fellow. With his salmon breast and grey and red head, rich brown shoulders and black, white brown and yellow sings he shouts for attention. Moreover, his song gives an added bonus, making his very attractive.

Nest of Goldfinch.

The Chaffinch

CHAPTER VII

THE BRAMBLEFINCH

A Bird Less Frequently Seen

AS a cage bird, the Bramblefinch is not quite such a favourite as the Chaffinch, possibly because he is not a British breeding species, and not quite so trustworthy with other birds.

Our specimens are obtained from the flocks that visit us during the winter months and leave early in the spring for their breeding quarters in Northern Europe. We are told that their nest is somewhat similar to that of the Chaffinch but a shade larger and not quite so neatly finished.

When in full colour these birds are very handsome and can generally hold their own against other Finches on the show bench. At fairly important shows they either have a class to themselves or compete against Chaffinches.

There are, no doubt, many bird lovers who would like to put up a pair for breeding and I would advise them to house the two birds in a fair-sized flight cage, giving them a nest box or other receptacle pushed into a bunch of birch twigs. Green moss, fine grass, a few feathers, vegetable down and broken up pieces of birch bark should be supplied.

The general treatment and feeding should be the same as for the Chaffinch, a bird which they closely resemble in many ways. The sexes are not difficult to distinguish, the cock being much brighter in plumage with an orange tawny breast ; the hen is appreciably duller and browner in colour.

Judging the Bramblefinch

These are attractive birds measuring 6½ ins. They are orange breasted with a shading of white surmounted by a darker colour of blue-black, and grey with a stippling of brown. The tail feathers are a greyish-black.

When judging it will be necessary to consider the colouring. Birds out of condition tend to lose the necessary lustre.

A mature bird, well-shaped and quite fit is likely to be the one to win.

The Bramblefinch

CHAPTER VIII

THE SISKIN

An Easily Tamed Variety : Essential Exercise
Live Food

THIS delightful little bird breeds much more extensively in Northern Europe than it does with us. It nests annually in Scotland and parts of Ireland, but our cage birds have been mostly obtained from the large flocks visiting us during the winter.

The sprightly Siskin is very popular as a cage bird, not only for exhibition, but also for breeding mules with the Canary, and choice hybrids with other Finches.

None of our small cage birds gets quite so tame and friendly as the Siskin. The bird lover can quickly get one to take a grain of Hemp seed from the fingers or come on to the hand for a choice morsel, and when once steadied it is equally at home in either cage or aviary.

That being so, there is no need to put wild specimens in an aviary when with a short period of caged life, and a little extra attention, they can be made so tame.

In this bird we have a species that can be greatly improved by careful selective breeding ; we can get them larger, with a more expansive bib and cap, and more even and richer in colour. The pencilling, a point in which many birds fail, we can improve and make sharply defined on both flanks.

Siskins take so readily to aviary and cage life that a pair will be quite happy and contented. I have had them escape from the aviary for a day or so, but they soon return and want to get in again.

In an aviary or large flight they will build a cosy nest, lay five or six eggs, and do their best to rear the young ones. For nesting purposes give them a couple of German Canary travelling cages, with two or three of the bars removed from one end. Surround these with a fir branch and the result is an almost natural site for them.

These birds have been bred in cages but do better in an aviary or large flight. In the latter the cock can be trusted with more confidence, and the extra exercise taken helps to keep them fit. They are otherwise very liable to put on fat and become heavy and lazy, so getting out of condition for a second nest.

Siskins should be fed very carefully. A plain diet of Canary, Rape and Teazle is best for them, with a little wild seed mixture for a change. A few grains of Hemp can be offered when getting them into breeding condition and when feeding the young, but otherwise this seed is too fattening.

All the usual seeding wild plants can be freely given, not forgetting seeding grass which is so useful when they are rearing young.

As a rule one has no trouble in getting these birds to take soft food. It should be a good insectile mixture in preference to hard-boiled egg and biscuit. They will eat the latter freely but it is not good for them.

Siskins will eat mealworms, small caterpillars, green fly and various other live food, and such food should be supplied if possible during the nesting period. Soaked seeds are also useful ; they make a change in the diet and if the birds will eat them freely they are better than soft food, although it is rather more trouble to keep up a constant supply.

For nest-building purposes Siskins should have fine roots, birch twigs, grass stalks, moss, vegetable down and hair.

The hen Siskin is easily distinguished from the cock ; she has not so much colour generally, is very much streaked and marked and has no black cap like the cock.

It is best to remove the young ones as soon as they can feed themselves, and gradually get them on to the usual seed mixture.

Judging the Siskin

Not as large as some of the earlier varieties, the Siskin is 4½ to 5ins in length. Moreover, although the mixture of black, predominant yellow and white is attractive, there are more striking birds. For this reason:

1. Colour — select mature birds which will be bright and attractive in colour. Preferably it should have a distinctive black cap.

2. Shape — ensure that the birds selected are very shapely.

3. Feathering — should be quite close and the yellowish-olive green should be bright and fresh.

Because of the likely competition from other species only a top-class Siskin should be shown.

The Siskin

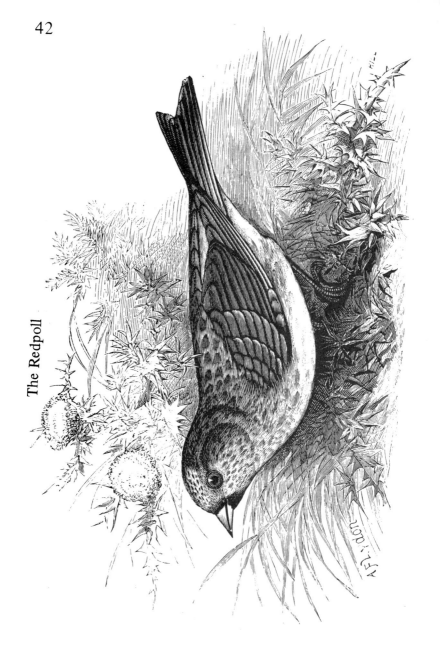

The Redpoll

CHAPTER IX

THE REDPOLL

The Two Species : Use of Cracked Hemp Field-Moulting and Sex

REDPOLLS are the most adaptable of all our Finches for breeding in aviaries, flights and cages. They have bred freely in these, and had it not been so easy to procure them from dealers they would, no doubt, have been more widely mated.

Although I have not seen a specimen of the cross, I believe the Lesser and the Mealy (or Greater) Redpoll have been paired, but I think myself that the two species should be kept quite distinct. They each have characteristics of their own that might be developed, and in each case more perfect show birds might well be evolved.

The Lesser Redpoll breeds mostly in Scotland and the North, but I am inclined to think that many nests are overlooked in the Southern Counties. I have found several myself on the wooded hills in Kent. It is a deep, beautifully rounded structure, somewhat smaller than that of the Linnet (for which it has probably been often mistaken) built of moss, fine twigs, roots and grass stalks, and smoothly lined with feathers, vegetable down, and hair.

Although the Redpoll usually has just the one nest in a season when at liberty, aviary-bred, well-fed birds are more prolific.

It is no trouble to get Redpoll hens to nest. They will build in a nest box, small wicker travelling cage, or coconut husk. Several of these should be hung about in various positions, and the birds allowed to make their choice.

Supply them with the building materials that they use in a wild state, and leave them as much as possible to themselves. If they are in an aviary or large flight they can usually be trusted to incubate the eggs and rear the young.

A stock seed mixture for them is the same as that supplied to the Linnet—that is, Canary 3 parts, Teazle 2 parts, Rape, Charlock and Linseed 1 part of each.

A little Hemp can be given in cold weather or when getting them into breeding condition, but it should be supplied in quite small quantities and lightly cracked, as it is rather a heavy task for a Redpoll with his small beak to break open such large seeds. Give wild seed mixture and the various seeding wild foods one can collect.

When rearing young a soft food of some kind should be supplied to the pairs. I know of some that were successfully reared last season on one of the well-known packet foods, and it is as well to supply them with a little soft food occasionally while building and incubating.

Baby Redpolls are very small when they leave the nest and one should see that the wires of the aviary or flight are securely fastened.

The sexing of Redpolls is not an easy matter, unless the birds are field-moulted. In that case the cock has a red breast and a richer colour on the rump. In house-moulted birds one can only trust to the song of the cock, with perhaps a shade more colour and blacker pencilling.

Judging Redpolls

There is considerable similarity between the Redpoll and the Linnet. The former is smaller (about 4¾ins) and has a darker marking at the point of the head in the male, although much ligher in the female.

Features to watch when judging are:

1. Colour — crown of head (poll) breast and rump as crimson as possible. The brown points should be quite distinct and bright. Should be quite mature.
2. Feathers — close and compact.
3. Tameness — steady on perch.

They are likeable characters and this should be evident from the friendly disposition shown by the birds.

CHAPTER X

THE TWITE

Deserving Greater Popularity : Care of the Young

THE Twite has never been quite so popular with southern fanciers as it deserves. It is true that it does not compare favourably with the Linnet as a songster, but it is a much prettier bird, having more colour and a greater variation in plumage.

Twites are northern birds, breeding in Scotland and the north of England. They come south in flocks during the

THE TWITE

winter months, mixing with the Linnets and others on the marshes and open fields.

In an aviary or large flight they will nest and rear their young if properly fed, for although they are seed-eaters they feed the young mostly on insects during the early stages. When they are due to hatch it is as well to supply them with a fair amount of green fly or any other live food that can be collected. Bunches of grasses will often contain live insects among the seeding tops, and a little soft food of good quality should not be forgotten.

The young are rather slow to mature and there should be no slackening of the proper food when they leave the nest; the cock should look after them while the hen prepares another home for a second clutch of eggs.

Keep them well supplied with nesting material, which should consist of fine roots, twigs of heather, wool, feathers, and vegetable down.

The sexes are easily distinguished, the cock having a reddish rump, which is absent in the hen.

Judging the Twite

Essential requirements are:

1. Size and shape — similar to the Linnet but smaller and more slender.
2. Colour — darker than the Linnet. Head well laced.
3. Feathering — sound and fine.
4. Steady in cage without any sign of wildness.

CHAPTER XI

THE HAWFINCH

Our Largest Finch : Shyness : Varying the Diet

MANY bird lovers will no doubt try to breed from a pair of our largest Finches, and there is no reason why they should not succeed.

Hawfinches have been produced on several occasions. In a wild state they are shy, retiring birds, particularly during the breeding season, and therefore some special precautions are necessary when getting them to nest in enclosures, and we must give them ample space, together with a certain amount of privacy.

They usually nest in a well-sheltered position in an orchard or among the dense branches of a fir, yew or holly, the nest resembling that of the Bullfinch, though somewhat larger. It is made of twigs, roots and grass stalks, and is lined with dry grass, fine roots and hair.

For breeding purposes a small aviary should be given up entirely to a pair of these birds, and a thick branch of fir, box or other evergreen should be fixed in one corner, with an old nest of any large species pushed into it.

For building, supply birch twigs, roots and the dry stalks of the wild plants given to the other Finches, dry grass and hair. Do not disturb the birds more than is absolutely necessary, particularly the sitting hen. Just give them food and water and leave them to themselves.

When at liberty the Hawfinch feeds upon seeds of all kinds, berries of the yew, hawthorn and others, nuts and beech masts, and insects of various kinds, particularly a smooth caterpillar found among the trees.

We must vary the diet of our aviary Hawfinches as much as possible. Their principal food will be Sunflower seed, of which they never appear to tire. It should be of the best quality, plump and firm with a good kernel inside. Offer also Canary, Hemp, Rape, Groats, Dari, Buckwheat and small Maize, various nuts, berries from the hedgerow and garden, green peas in the pod, ripe apple and pear, a little Watercress, Chickweed and Shepherd's-Purse.

For soft food give a good brand of insectile mixture. Get them if possible to take this pretty freely as it will be very helpful when the young appear. They must then have mealworms, grubs, caterpillars, small worms and live ants' eggs, and a little Sunflower seed and Hemp just sprouting.

The hen Hawfinch may be as large as the cock bird but is not so rich in colour; the crown of the head is ashy brown, with chocolate colour at the back, while as a rule the black bib at the throat is scarcely so large as that of the cock.

The Hawfinch

Judging the Hawfinch

The Hawfinch is a large bird (7ins) with a massive bill. Provided the size and condition are good the aim should be to select birds which excel in the following:

1. Colour — rich brown head with a white collar; back and shoulders dark brown; breast a lighter brown; black at front of each eye and on throat.

2. Feathering — compact and sound with a neat appearance.

3. Alertness.

Food Hopper for holding around 6lb of canary seed (Courtesy: Haines Aviary Economy).

Grosbeak or Hawfinch.

CHAPTER XII

THE YELLOW BUNTING

A Favourite Pet : Use of Ants' Eggs

THE Yellow Bunting or Yellow Hammer has always been a favourite with bird lovers both as a singing pet and for exhibition purposes. Young Buntings get tame and familiar readily, and for that reason would be best for breeding purposes.

I have found that old birds, even when fairly steady in a cage, tend to become nervous if turned into an aviary or large flight.

The Yellow Bunting is a common bird of the countryside, easily recognised, and is familiar along every lane and hedgerow of the open country. It can be found in cultivated fields and stubbles, where in the winter it consorts with the Sparrows, Greenfinches and others, visiting the farmyards in very severe weather.

Its food is grain and seeds of all kinds and in the summer, when rearing the young, insects and caterpillars are added to the bill of fare. Very probably the young are fed chiefly upon live food during the first few days of their existence.

The nest of the Yellow Bunting is usually built on or near the ground, and is a rather bulky construction, but beautifully finished and rounded internally. The nests differ a good deal in the material used externally, all those that I have seen (and they are many) having been most neatly finished inside with fine roots and hair.

When put up for breeding in the aviary or flight it would be best to give them a rough gorse branch with the coarse grass or heather twisted among it and the whole fastened into a corner, or placed upon the ground.

Let them have fine roots, coarse grass that has been pulled up by the roots and allowed to dry, moss, short lengths of dry grass, and hair.

Although the Yellow Bunting will live for a long time on Canary seed only, it is as well to encourage it to take other seeds so as to give some variety to its diet. One can offer a little Rape, lightly-cracked Hemp, coarse Groats, Maw and some wild seed mixture.

It is necessary to give Buntings a little live food occasionally, and it will have to be supplied freely when the young are first hatched. For this purpose we require mealworms, gentles, flies, small beetles and grubs generally.

One of the best foods we can give these birds is live ants' eggs, but of course it is not every bird-keeper who can procure them. The next best is some dried ones of good quality ; soak them in a little new milk, drain them on a cloth, and give in a small dish on the top of a little good insectile food.

If you can get them to take a small quantity of the latter regularly it will help considerably in the feeding.

These birds are not particularly keen on green food, although they will nibble a little occasionally and will pick over a bunch of wild food and seeding grass.

The hen Yellow Bunting is not so rich in colour as the cock. She is more greyish green and has only a tinge of yellow on the head and cheeks. Generally she is the more spotted.

The Yellow Bunting (Yellow Hammer)

Judging the Yellow Bunting
(Yellow Hammer)

The bright yellow head and mixture of brown, orange, black and blue make these birds quite attractive.

They reach a length of around 6¼ins but are relatively slim when compared with the Bullfinch or Goldfinch.

For showing it is advisable to select mature birds of two or three years old, noting the following:

1. Colour – as bright as possible.

2. Feathering – fine and silky without any roughness or breakage.

3. Condition – must be in top condition without trace of wildness.

Canary Seed   White Millet   Japanese Millet

Typical Canary Seeds

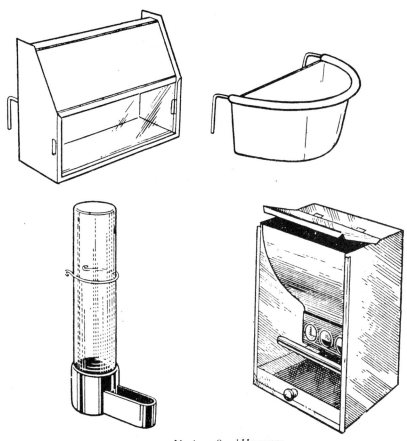

Various Seed Hoppers

CHAPTER XIII

THE CORN BUNTING

Care in Breeding : Canary Seed : Coaxing to Other Food

THE Corn Bunting is the largest of the family, and is fairly common in all open cultivated districts. It is a big handsome bird, but not a general favourite as a household pet, although as a fancier's bird it takes a prominent position and good specimens of both sexes are seldom out of the money prizes at the shows. Frequently they have taken the special prize as the best bird in the British section.

No doubt some bird lover will try to breed from a pair ; if so they should be fairly steady and must have a small aviary or flight to themselves. They are inclined to be quarrelsome and could not be kept with other birds during the breeding season.

The Corn Bunting nests on the ground, generally among tall grass or corn or under the shelter of a bush on a bank. I would advise a small bundle of twigs, with coarse grass and herbage mixed with it, pushed into a corner of the aviary or flight. The rougher and more natural this could be made to appear the better.

As nesting material offer dry grass, fine roots, " twitch " grass pulled up by the roots, moss and a little hair.

In a state of freedom Corn Buntings must feed upon a variety of seeds and insects, but when caged the only seed that appeals to them and of which they never tire is Canary, which is probably the nearest approach to grass seed. Of course, there is much more in it, and possibly it is rather more tasty.

Anyway, whatever the attraction is, it is the one and only seed worth having as far as a Corn Bunting is concerned !

Although Canary must be their stock seed it is as well to offer others, but only in small quantities to pick over and select what they fancy. Give small Oats, Rape, Charlock, wild seed mixture, cracked Hemp, Maw, and Linseed.

They will eat mealworms, flies, gentles, small beetles and grubs generally. Live ants' eggs are greatly appreciated, but, failing these, procure some best quality dry ones and soak them in fresh milk, as advised for the Yellow Bunting.

When they will take these pretty freely, it is only another step to get them to eat a good brand of insectile mixture which would be the stock food for rearing purposes.

There is very little difference in the sexes, the hen usually being somewhat smaller, less bold in head, and more effeminate looking generally. It is thought that they pair for life so it is as well not to part a likely looking couple even if they fail the first season.

Judging the Corn Bunting

Since this is the larger of the Buntings the judge will expect to see a good sized bird (7ins) and weighing around 2oz.

Besides the overall size, which includes a broad head, the bird should excel in colour with good, strong markings.

The Corn Bunting

CHAPTER XIV

THE CIRL BUNTING

A Handsome Specimen

THE Cirl Bunting is one of the most attractive of the Bunting family. It is not so generally distributed as the others, being more a bird of the southern counties, and probably not quite so hardy.

The cock is a very handsome fellow ; he has a chestnut breast and yellow abdomen. His head is olive green, his throat black, his back rich chestnut streaked with black.

The hen is without the black and yellow markings on the face, the throat and breast are striped, and the lesser wing coverts are greenish grey, which is different from the colour of the back.

The Cirl Bunting is a somewhat shy bird and yet has been bred in captivity. To do this successfully a small aviary given up to a pair would be needed, and it should be in a sheltered, warm situation.

When free, this species builds close to the ground in a thicket of briars and bramble or a gorse bush, or maybe in a hedge bank among the coarse herbage and roots.

We can supply the gorse bush and the rough stuff in the aviary, and give them fine roots, dry grass, leaves, coarse grass with roots, and a little moss and hair.

Like all the other Buntings the Cirl is quite content with an unlimited supply of sound Canary seed, but other seeds in small quantities should be offered, and one should be rather more liberal with mealworms and other insects.

Insectile food with an extra allowance of sound ants' eggs mixed with it should be offered pretty freely, as it will lessen the need for quite so much live food. It will be upon these two that the successful rearing of the young will mainly depend.

Should the young leave the nest during a cold spell it would be as well to catch them up and keep them comfortable for a time, as they are very susceptible to sudden changes in temperature.

THE CIRL BUNTING

Judging the Cirl Bunting

For success it is necessary to select a well coloured specimen, with close and compact feathering which is not broken in any way.

CHAPTER XV

THE REED BUNTING

Favourite Haunts

THE only other member of the Bunting family that bird lovers would be likely to try and breed would be the Reed Bunting, a very attractive species and as active and interesting as any of the family.

This bird is usually found near streams and tidal rivers where tall reeds and coarse herbage grow abundantly. But favourite haunts where I have found several nests are disused brick and clay pits.

On the edge of these reeds, long coarse grass, and other vegetation grow quickly, and a pair of these birds will soon take possession when the workmen have gone and the place is quiet.

The nest is usually on the ground or just a few inches above it in a clump of rushes or strong growing grass. It is a rather untidy affair and at first glance looks not unlike a heap of rubbish, made as it is of dry grass, withered reeds and rushes, a bit of moss, in fact any flexible, soft vegetation to be found close by. Internally it is finished off with finer grass, hair and usually some dry flowers of the reeds.

A large flight would be quite suitable for a pair of these birds, with a bundle of twigs and rough vegetation such as one could easily collect near a stream or pond.

With these as a foundation and a good supply of material for building, these birds should soon get to work. They are early in pairing and being double-brooded would have the long summer days to rear more than one nest. They are very devoted to the young and should make good parents.

The Reed Bunting should be fed in the same manner as the other Buntings, that is, Canary seed as the staple diet, with a little of other seeds as a change, ants' eggs, insectile food, and insects, the latter mostly when breeding and rearing young.

The sexes are easily distinguished as the hen lacks the black head and throat and has no yellow tinge on the under part of the body.

Judging the Reed Bunting

Some bird fanciers prefer to show hens, the belief being that these are more easily trained, but there is no real evidence to support this view.

The advantage of showing a cock of two or three years old is that he will be larger and with the black head is more striking.

Perfect plumage is essential and for a bird to win he or she should be very fit condition and quite tame.

The Reed Bunting

CHAPTER XVI

BREEDING SOFTBILLS

General Hints : Modern Puppy and Chicken Meals Cheese : Ants' Eggs : Wasp Grubs : Mealworms Other Live Food

THE keeping of softbilled birds in aviaries and cages is not so difficult a matter now that it used to be some years ago.

In those far-off days little was known about the actual requirements of softbills, especially the migrants. They were simply looked upon as insect eaters, and unsuitable, if not impossible, to keep in cages for any length of time. Now, however, we know that their successful maintenance is simply a matter of suitable accommodation and proper feeding.

In looking back, we are apt to wonder how it was that so many of our pet softbills survived, but on probing into the matter we should discover that it was the hardier species which were kept, such as Magpies, Jays, Thrushes, Blackbirds and Larks, birds that when once settled down will thrive upon almost anything that a bird can eat.

At that time the principal foods in use were bread and crushed Hemp seed or bruised Rape, raw meat, egg and bread.

A particular favourite was a certain concoction termed " German paste ", the main ingredients of which were pea meal, dripping, wheat meal and honey, the whole cooked until it was a golden brown. This was given to Blackbirds, Thrushes and Larks, the latter appearing to thrive on it, possibly because their digestive organs are fairly strong !

Nowadays, however, bird keepers and vendors of foods have used their brains to some purpose, so that we have ready to hand quite a long list of nutritious and eminently suitable foods.

For the larger birds we can use puppy meals and crushed puppy biscuits, best quality chicken meals, and some of the excellent foods put up by well-known firms in packet form ready for immediate use.

For the more delicate migrant softbills we have the superfine insectile foods which can be purchased at most dealers and bird shops, or obtained direct from the makers. Although these vary slightly in the ingredients used, most of them contain ants' eggs, dried flies, silkworm pupæ, desiccated yolk of egg, with ground biscuit or sponge cake.

Another great help to successful softbill keeping is that we can these days obtain fresh fruit all the year round. Many birds will eat freely of this and thrive upon it, and it is a splendid natural corrective to the dried ants' eggs, flies and so forth.

Currants and Sultanas

Then occasionally we can make use of grocer's currants and sultanas. These should be first washed in warm water, strained off and gently rubbed in a cloth. They can be added to the staple food or given separately. Some birds get so fond of them that they waste the staple food hunting for them, so that the latter method is probably better.

Another very nutritious food, and one that is always to hand, is cheese. Some good sound Cheddar or Gloster scraped or grated and mixed with the usual food makes a welcome change.

Cream cheese can also be made use of ; this is, perhaps, better suited to the more delicate species, but the hardier ones will not refuse it.

All softbills need live food and the more delicate they are the more they need. I have, however, kept some of the commoner and hardier species for months without any, giving instead a tiny morsel of raw lean meat. If this is quite fresh, it will do no harm, used judiciously ; it takes the place of the live food and satisfies the bird's natural craving for a change from the usual stock mixture.

During the summer months it is possible for bird keepers

who live in the country to procure their own fresh ants' eggs, which are much more valuable as food than the very best of the dried variety, and are just the tit-bit required when the young softbills are hatched.

The ant-hill can be opened and a shovelful of the contents dropped into an airtight box, to be later emptied on the floor of the aviary for the birds to help themselves, taking their fill of insects and eggs. Alternatively they can be collected and doled out to the birds as required.

A good way to collect them is to choose a sunny day, and lay a sheet of paper on the ground near the anthill. The hill should then be opened with a shovel or small spade and the ants will carry the eggs to the shelter of the paper, when they can be carefully collected and put in boxes or bags and taken home.

When disturbed the ants are furious and care must be taken not to get them on the hands, or on one's boots and socks. It is advisable to wear an old pair of boots that can be greased or treated with some strong disinfectant.

Any surplus ants' eggs can be dried in a moderate oven and stored for future use.

Wasp Grubs

Wasp grubs form a valuable addition to the birds' diet, and can generally be purchased at a naturalist's store. The hardy and expert fancier may feel inclined to attempt the rather hazardous business of getting them direct from a nest, but it is important to remember that, apart from the personal risk involved, the use of an insecticide may render the grubs poisonous.

Of all the insects and live food that we can collect, none is quite so useful as the mealworm. This is our staple insect food, procurable at almost any time and not objectionable to handle. All birds will eat mealworms, even the Finches, who live mostly on a seed diet, but they should be given with a certain amount of discretion because the hard, thick skins are rather indigestible. Thus the larger mealworms should be used for the more robust birds and the small ones for the more delicate species.

Bird-keepers who have several softbills should breed their own mealworms, at least in sufficient quantity to help the supply. Many years ago I used to get mine from an old mill. I was allowed to hunt around in dark corners and odd places, and sometimes made a big find among some old sacks.

Mealworms turn up when least expected. For a time I kept some softbills in an outhouse, while a proper bird room was being constructed, and some months later I found quite a quantity of worms and beetles in that shed. Some of the mealworms had escaped from the birds and established themselves in a corner, there breeding and multiplying.

Breeding Mealworms

To breed them under control is not a difficult matter, but some patience is required. There are several methods, of which the following is as good as any :—

Procure a couple of rather flat wooden boxes about two feet square, and make lids to fit with a flange all round them to prevent the mealworms escaping. Cut a hole in the centre about three inches square and cover this with a piece of fine perforated zinc (this is for ventilation). Cut some coarse sacking twice the size of the floor space of the box, so that when folded it fits inside closely but not tightly.

Put into the box a layer of crushed Oats, Bran and meal, about an inch and a half thick, then the folded sacks, and on this a sheet of coarse brown paper. Another layer of the Oats and meal follows, more sacking and paper, then more meal, and this should be continued until the box is three parts full. Then turn in a pint or so of mealworms.

Some breeders soak the paper and one or two of the sacks in beer and treacle, allowing it to dry in well before using. The boxes should now be placed in a fairly warm position, such as a cupboard near a fireplace, under the hot-water pipes of a greenhouse, or in some similar location.

They should be left undisturbed for some months as it takes about a year for the worms to change to beetles, and the beetles to lay the eggs that hatch and produce the worms again.

Sometimes during the summer months one is able to obtain the beetles, and if so this shortens the period of production considerably. Occasionally a new box should be started from the contents of the old one, a job best carried out in the winter.

In addition to the live food named, there is a good deal that can be collected by the keen bird-keeper, such as house flies, beetles, caterpillars, earwigs, green fly, small earth worms, maggots and others.

SHOWING SOFTBILLS

Unlike the seedeaters which tend to use standard type show cages of a specified size (pro rata to type of bird) the softbills may have to be "staged" so that they are exhibited in what appears to be natural surroundings. In other words cages are decorated with suitable interiors:

1. Very small birds; eg wrens, titmice, use a little foliage such as fir or ivy, with natural twigs as perches.

2. Medium size birds; eg Warblers, Nightingales, where more foliage is recommended, although not too much or the birds cannot be seen. Heathers, small stumps, beech sprays, laurel, etc. may be used. Birds such as the Reed Bunting might have rushes or reeds in the cage.

3. Large softbills such as Magpies, Jays and Thrushes should have large undecorated cages (eg 30L x 20H x 14W [inches]).

The size of cage to use and the painting is laid down and must be followed.

The rules regarding each can be obtained from the appropriate cage bird society, eg. Budgerigar Society, Southern Norwich Plainhead Canary Club.

The fact that birds have to be trained must be recognised, but, since the standard show cages are quite small, each lesson should be relatively short.

Daily training in small cages should be restricted to one hour per day and visits to shows should not exceed 72 hours.

CHAPTER XVII

MAGPIES, JAYS, AND JACKDAWS

A Quiet Corner : The Magpies' Nest : Feeding and Nest Material

THE two largest of our softbills that any bird-keeper would be likely to try and breed with are the Magpie and Jay.

Both species are well worth keeping. They are not only particularly handsome but very interesting and make most delightful pets. They are splendid mimics, and if kept in a suitable garden enclosure are cheerful and entertaining.

To breed with a pair with any hope of success a fair-sized aviary would have to be given up to them, and the prospective parents should be young birds if possible.

In a wild state they are very secretive and wily in their nesting, and therefore some attempt should be made to enable them to nest in seclusion. A good thick bush of faggots might be placed in one corner of the aviary, and if a board can be fastened up to screen it partly, so much the better. The birds will appreciate this quiet corner.

Magpies must be supplied with quite a quantity of sticks of various kinds ; some thorn branches should be included as these are the favourites, and most used for the roof or dome of the nest.

These sticks are cemented together with mud and clay, so a lump of clay in a shallow pan of water will be welcomed. When the nest is well on the way supply plenty of fine fibrous roots for the lining.

The only difference in the sexes that I have noticed is the slightly smaller size of the hen bird, and her plumage is not quite so lustrous, especially in the spring and early summer, when the cock looks at his best.

A similar bush or bundle of faggots should be given to the Jays in their aviary, but in their case some evergreens, such as holly or yew, should be included. The nest will be formed externally of twigs and sticks and lined with fibrous roots.

Both Magpies and Jays can be fed upon a good brand of chicken meal, as used to rear young chicks, pheasant meal or crushed puppy biscuits made crumbly moist with hot water, or a little gravy for a change. Give scraps from the table such as suet, rice and other puddings, boiled potatoes and vegetables, brown bread and milk, occasionally a very little lean meat, smashed nuts, acorns, wheat, fruit and berries of various kinds, a freshly killed mouse, beetles, caterpillars, mealworms and other live food.

A pair of Jackdaws can be fed in the same way. For breeding they would need an aviary to themselves and a good-sized nest box with an entrance hole at the side would possibly suit them as well as anything. This could be covered roughly with virgin cork to give it some resemblance to a tree trunk.

The nesting material for these birds will be almost anything that they can carry, but it is as well to supply them with sticks, straw, hay, long grass, clods pulled up by the roots, moss, wool and feathers.

The difference in the sexes is that the hen is rather smaller than the cock and the grey collar is not quite so clear and distinct.

Jackdaw

Magpie

Jay

CHAPTER XVIII

THE SONG THRUSH

Our Most Popular Softbill

THE most popular bird among softbills is, no doubt, the Song Thrush—a big, bold, handsome fellow whose spotted breast and intelligent eye makes him conspicuous among others. He is not only noted for his beauty of form and feather, but as a musician he takes high rank.

He is a constant performer, singing in the spring and early summer from daylight till dusk, and he is generally the last of the feathered choir to be heard. Little wonder that he is such a prime favourite and so much in demand as a caged pet.

As an exhibition bird he is splendid, usually fearless and showing himself to perfection when being judged. But as he needs a fair-sized cage which is not easily conveyed any distance, we do not see so many of them at exhibitions as we should like.

The Song Thrush has bred in captivity and I feel sure that a good many will be produced in the future. A pair of young birds should be selected and should be caged some time before they are turned into an aviary or large flight.

The Nest Site

A rough bundle of branches with evergreens intermixed should be placed in a suitable position. They would make no fuss about building in this, as when free their nest has been constructed in all sorts of positions. I have found it myself in evergreens, heaps of rough branches in a faggot stack, against a wall, just supported by a branch or two of ivy, even on the ground and the top of a bank.

If an old nest can be found and pushed into the centre of the bundle it would encourage them. The material supplied for nest-making should be plenty of twigs and dry grass, a little moss and dead leaves. When this is worked into shape a lining of mud will be put in, and into this some wet rotten wood.

The Mud Lining

The mud for lining can be supplied by having a shallow pan of water with a lump of clay in it, and a small decayed branch will give them all the wood they require. In hot, dry summers I have noticed that the mud lining is sometimes omitted ; this may be due to the scarcity of mud, or perhaps to the birds' instinct telling them that it is not needed for warmth.

The hen is a close sitter and even when at liberty will allow one to pass quite close to the nest. If you pretend not to see her she appears quite content and has no thought of danger while incubating. Should she be used to you, you can do almost anything with the young when they are hatched. I have frequently given nestlings a small worm with the mother Thrush a few feet away looking on interestedly.

The feeding of the Song Thrush is not a very difficult matter ; soft food is needed, with fruit and insects. The soft food can consist of a good brand of chicken meal— not the kind given to adult birds, but that used for the rearing of young chicks. This should be made crumbly moist with hot water. Sometimes a little hard-boiled egg or a few ants' eggs can be added to it.

Another good food is crushed puppy biscuits, and then there are the excellent foods put up in packets by well-known firms. Thus a suitable staple diet is not at all a difficult matter to provide. Fruit can be offered in season and live food in moderation ; for if one is too liberal it becomes a necessity to them, and they go soft if the usual quantity is not always on hand.

It is a little difficult to distinguish the cocks and hens ; one is able to distinguish the cock more by manner,

Song Thrush

carriage and actions than by any special marking. The following hints may be useful : The back of the cock is darker and more glossy, the markings round the throat are better defined, the breast colour is richer and the underparts are whiter, with the tips on the wing coverts rather larger and a sharper colour. But the cock is such a splendid songster that it is not long before he proclaims his sex if he is in good health.

A Morning Bath (from an old print)

CHAPTER XIX

THE BLACKBIRD

A Ready Nester

PRESSING the Song Thrush hard for popularity as a pet softbill is the Blackbird, a splendid fellow with his glossy black coat and golden bill. A glorious songster well known to everybody, he sings at his best when his mate is sitting within hearing on her clutch of bluish-green eggs, mottled with reddish-brown.

The Blackbird is not quite such an early nester as the Song Thrush, being more of a late spring bird, and I am doubtful if he is quite so hardy as the Thrush, although quite able to stand the winter in an outside enclosure.

For breeding in an aviary or large flight young birds should be chosen. These can be distinguished by the reddish tinge to the primary wing feathers, which are not dead black until after the second moult. The hen has a brown beak, is not so black generally as the cock, and is mottled on the breast.

There should be no difficulty in getting these birds to nest in a bush of branches and evergreens, as the latter are favourites with them in a wild state. They also go for sites along the hedgerow where rough trimmings have been pushed into a gap for repairs.

In fact they are not at all particular as to the location of their home; the most unlikely place will often take their fancy, so with a little encouragement they should build in a bush in the aviary.

Supply the pair with plenty of dry grass, a few twigs and moss, and the nest they build they will plaster inside with mud and afterward line it with more dry grass.

The stock food advised for the Thrush suits the Blackbird quite well, but one should occasionally add a portion of insectile food to it, giving also a little more live food, especially when getting them into breeding condition.

The Blackbird eats more fruit than the Thrush and should have his share of anything that is in season, such as sweet cherries, currants, strawberries, raspberries, apples and pears, both of the latter given a bit over-ripe.

It will be advisable to improve the stock food a little when the young first arrive. This can be done by the addition of a little insectile food or hard-boiled yolk of egg well mixed into the food with a fork.

The young birds should be caged off as soon as they can feed themselves as they are inclined to be quarrelsome.

THE BLACKBIRD.

CHAPTER XX

THE STARLING

"Life Partners" : The Nest Site

STARLINGS pair for life, so any bird lover who intends to breed with a pair should begin with young birds, and keep them together for the years that they are in good health.

These birds like to nest under cover ; they select holes in trees, walls and old buildings. A colony of them will take possession of a barn roof or church steeple, and rear numbers of young ones. They are very prolific and will continue to lay clutch after clutch until the autumn moult puts them out of action.

A pair should do well in a big flight. A wooden box for nesting should be about 18 inches square with a hole in one side for entrance, or one side could simply be left open and have a piece of board nailed across at the bottom to keep the nesting material in place.

This arrangement would allow more light to the interior, and would facilitate cleaning it out when necessary.

The nesting box should be left in the flight all the year round as the old birds frequently visit the nesting site and roost in it, and they will be ready to start again early the next season.

One need not be particular about the building materials supplied ; straw, grass and fine roots would perhaps be the best, with a few feathers for lining.

The hen Starling is, as a rule, rather heavier in build than the cock, and is more profusely spotted ; these spots are somewhat larger, which gives her a lighter appearance. The cock bird is smarter, rather richer in colour, and has more sheen on his plumage.

The young birds until the moult are quite unlike the parents, being a brownish-grey colour all over except on the breast and underparts, which are white.

The Starling

CHAPTER XXI

OTHER SOFTBILL SPECIES

Care of the Smaller Varieties

BIRD-KEEPERS need not confine their breeding of softbills to the larger species only, several of the smaller and equally beautiful birds having at various times been bred.

The smaller examples are, if anything, more valuable as cage birds, both as singing pets and for exhibition purposes. In the bird room they can be kept in smaller flights and cages and are much more easily conveyed to and from the shows.

Among a few of the species that have been bred are Larks, Pipits, Spotted Flycatchers, Hedge Sparrows and Bearded Reedlings. If these can be successfully reared there is no reason why several others should not. In the case of Skylarks these have been bred in an ordinary cage of reasonable length, when they made their nest in a hollowed turf.

A long flight would be quite suitable for a pair, with a turf at one end hollowed in the middle, this cavity being surrounded by a handful or two of coarse herbage to give a little shelter.

Skylarks are not difficult birds to feed. The same soft food as given to the larger species will meet their needs, with a spoonful of insectile food in it when getting them into condition, or feeding young. A little chopped hard-boiled egg could be added for a change.

They will eat various seeds and green food and should have a mealworm or two, live ants' eggs, grubs and earwigs.

The cock is usually a larger, bolder, more upstanding bird than the hen, with longer wings.

Another glorious songster is the Woodlark, and a pair of these might be treated in much the same manner as the Skylark ; but I have found them to be rather more delicate feeders and to require a little better stock mixture.

They usually nest on the ground, but not in such open situations as the Skylark ; in a flight, however, the same arrangements for nesting should be suitable. Dried grass, moss and cow hair are the materials used in constructing the nest.

The Hedge Sparrow, in my opinion, has been very much neglected as a cage bird. The cock is not to be despised as a songster, for although he has little variety in his song, it is sweet and soft and has a joyous ring.

As an exhibition bird he has, unfortunately, had to compete with rarer and more attractively coloured soft-bills for premier honours, but I see no reason why in the future these birds should not have a class to themselves at some of the larger shows.

THE PIPIT

The cock in full plumage is a decidedly attractive bird, and as the species would breed freely in flights, from an exhibition standpoint these birds would soon be very much improved by careful selection of stock. They are very hardy, and may be kept under almost any conditions.

Hedge Sparrows nest early in the year, usually before there are any leaves on the hedgerows and bushes, and so one frequently finds a nesting site in a heap of hedge trimmings or branches. Thus it should take readily to a small bundle of evergreens and branches in a flight.

The birds will need to be supplied with fine roots, dead grass, moss, and wool, hair and feathers for the nest lining ; the finished article is a charming little house, and when filled with its clutch of clear blue eggs possesses a beauty all its own'.

BEARDED REEDLINGS
The difference in the sexes is well-marked, the hen being the left-hand bird of this pair

Another reason why the Hedge Sparrow should be a popular breeding species is the ease with which it can be fed. It should have a good brand of chick meal made moist, various seeds including a wild mixture, and a mealworm or two occasionally. In the breeding season the soft food could be varied by the addition of a little meat meal, chopped suet or hard-boiled egg. Fruit, berries and seeding wild plants should be offered. During the winter months it will do quite well on the soft food and seeds.

Among the rarer softbills Bearded Reedlings have been reared in a good-sized aviary, the parents being fed upon insectile food with an extra allowance of ants' eggs and occasionally a little hard-boiled yolk of egg. Various seeds including Maw were also given.

No doubt other species could also be encouraged to breed, especially those that consume a good deal of fruit in their diet, such as the Blackcap and Garden Warbler.

Nest of Hedge Sparrow.

CHAPTER XXII

HAND REARING

The Best Time to Start : A "Feeding Stick"

THERE may be times when the parent birds refuse
to feed the young or carry out their duties in such
a half-hearted manner that the bird-keeper might decide
to rear them himself.

Young Finches can be reared by good feeding hen
Canaries, and the babies need not always have been
hatched out by their foster-parents.

For instance, a nest of young Goldfinches about three
days old was found in an apple tree. The chicks were
taken home and given to a pair of Canaries, whose own
eggs were removed. The whole brood was successfully
reared on the same food as given to rear young Canaries.

Young British birds can be reared at any age. I have
reared them myself from three days old and also finished
them off from a fortnight to three weeks. But given the
choice of the time to start rearing it should be just as
the eyes begin to open. The nest with the brood in it
should be put into a shallow box and covered with flannel
for warmth, unless it is thought to be advisable to leave
the nest for the parent birds to start another family.

In this case a nest should be made in the box, an ordinary
lined nest-pan being used with a little moss and hair, and
if these are worked round with the hand quite a good nest
can be formed.

The soft foods for rearing will vary somewhat, according
to the species, but personally I prefer hard-boiled egg and
Osborne biscuits for this job. The egg should be boiled

for ten minutes. When cold, well mix with a fork the yolk and part of the white into two crushed Osborne biscuits, and to this add a dessert-spoonful of best ants' eggs, free from rubbish.

There are several other foods, normally intended to rear Canaries, that can be used, but I find that not all of them are quite so satisfactory to handle, since they are apt to fall off the feeding stick while being used.

Making a Feeding Stick

A feeding stick, by the way, can be made out of a flat stick, shaping it with a knife to about three-sixteenths of an inch at one end, and, of course, flat so that the food will stay on. The point should be rounded.

Take a little of the mixture and make the food fairly wet with fresh new milk ; get a scrap on the stick, and when the birds gape for food (which they will do directly you touch them) put the mixture well into the mouth, but be careful not to injure the sensitive lining or the tongue.

Feed a little at a time, and often, according to the age of the birds ; the younger they are the more frequently they must be fed. Once every hour is a general rule, gradually increasing the time to every two hours as they grow.

The very first feed in the morning should be a small one, after which the nestlings appear to wake up and will then take a larger quantity. During the day they do not need much, but about four o'clock in the afternoon you can begin to pack them with food for the night so that they go to sleep with full crops.

Warmth and Cleanliness

It is important that the brood be kept warm and clean. If it is a large one they naturally make each other warm, but if there are only one or two, they should be well covered up with a layer of flannel, and put near a hot-water pipe at night.

As soon as they begin to sit on the edge of the nest or get out of it, they should be removed to a cage, the nest placed in one corner, and some soft food put on the floor of the cage.

When mealtime comes, try to feed them from the pan of food and encourage them to peck at it. As soon as one starts feeding the others will quickly follow.

When they can feed themselves, still continue to give them soft food until they can crack seed, and even then give them a little occasionally, letting them have it fairly dry.

When hand-rearing softbills, in addition to the soft food, a few ants' eggs should be dropped into the mouth with a small pair of tweezers, and they can also be given tiny mealworms or parts of the larger ones dipped in milk.

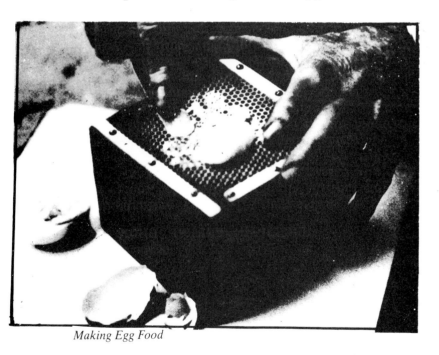

Making Egg Food

INCUBATION PERIODS

As a *guide* to the period required for incubation the following table is given:

Species	Period (Days)	Eggs	Nesting Material
†Goldfinch	13	4	Grass, moss, wool
*Bullfinch	14	4	Roots with hair lining
Linnet	12	4	Grass and moss
†Greenfinch	13	4	Twigs, moss, wool
*Chaffinch	13	4	Moss, grass
*Bramblefinch	14	6	Grass, moss, feathers
†Siskin	13	4	Twigs, moss
†Redpoll	13	4	Roots, stalks, feathers
Twite	12	5	Grass and moss
†Hawfinch	14	4	Grass, twigs, plants
*Yellow Bunting	13	4	Grass, straw, moss
*Corn Bunting	13	4	Grass, straw, moss
*Cirl Bunting	14	4	Dried grass, hair
*Reed Bunting	14	4	Grass and hair
Magpies	17	6	Sticks, mud, grass
Jays	17	5	Sticks, twigs
Jackdaws	18	4	Sticks, wool, hair
Song Thrush	14	4	Grass, roots, leaves
Blackbird	14	4	Grass, moss, mud
Starling	13	5	Straw, grass

† Very sociable so will breed with other birds present
* May prefer single pair in aviary for breeding or must be kept separated, eg Bullfinch.

The period may vary by a day and the normal clutch is given. The nest may be on a platform of twigs and is often lined with hair, wool or feathers (depending on the species).

The aim should be to provide conditions which come near to those found in the wild, eg, bushes in aviary, suitable nest boxes and material likely to be used for making the nest.

CHAPTER XXIII

RINGING THE YOUNG BIRDS

How to Fit Closed Rings

FOR many years now it has been the custom for breeders of Canaries, Hybrids and British birds to mark their young stock by means of rings placed on the leg for identification purposes. These rings are made to clip round the shank of the bird just as it leaves the nest, and can easily be removed at any time if it becomes necessary.

In some Societies closed rings are placed on birds intended for competition, for certain cups and trophies. These rings must be put on the birds while they are still in the nest, and if removed afterwards they cannot be refitted. Under the provisions of the *Wildlife and Countryside Act, 1981*, it is necessary to *close-ring* all cage- and aviary-bred British birds intended for sale, or for exhibition. The best plan, is to close-ring *all* young birds bred in captivity, thus keeping within the law.

When to Ring

The rings used for most of the Finches will be of the same size as are now in use for Canaries and Hybrids. The Hawfinch, Buntings, Larks, Blackbirds and Thrushes would naturally need rings somewhat larger. It is impossible to give the exact age for putting on the rings, but usually it is from six to nine days. A Greenfinch, for instance, with its larger feet would need to be rung a day or so earlier than a Goldfinch or Redpoll. There is a risk of the ring slipping off if put on too soon, and if left too late it is somewhat difficult to get on.

When ringing is left rather late the ring may be warmed in hot water, when the slight expansion caused will help to make fitting easy. The rings should be laid out all ready, so that there is no fuss or flurry over the operation. Take the baby bird in the left hand so that you have the leg and foot quite free ; slip the ring carefully over the three front claws, then over the ball of the foot, and up the shank, taking the hind claw with it. When it is past the claw, it can be released and the job is completed.

The best time to carry out ringing is in the evening, as the old bird will settle down on the young when they are returned without being too inquisitive. It is a good plan to have a nice big bunch of seeding wild food to offer to the birds, not only to entice the hen off the nest but also to keep them busy while you are ringing the nestlings.

The British Bird Council supplies close rings of varying sizes and a list may be obtained from them.* These are given a code letter: eg "A" for wrens, willow warblers, goldcrests, and "W" for such birds as Goshawks and Marsh Harriers.

For exhibition purposes a bird must be ringed and, therefore, the reulations relating to the show must be followed.

Split rings are also available and these may be fitted on the bird by using special pliers. Again different sizes should be used to comply with the requirement of the bird.

*Since the address changes, interested parties should contact the RSPB, Sandy, Beds.